LILY & NANA
a book about laughing and loving!

Lily Hamilton ♡ *Barbara Myers*

by **Lily Hamilton** & **Barbara Myers**

illustrated by **Brendon Sellaro**

Headline Kids
an imprint of **Headline Books, Inc.**

Terra Alta, WV

Dedication

Lily and Nana are proud to dedicate some of the proceeds from the sale of this book to the Monongalia County Child Advocacy Center. The Monongalia County Child Advocacy center is a nonprofit organization dedicated to serving victims of child abuse by providing a child-friendly, safe environment where children and their families can be interviewed, educated and healed.

Lily & Nana

by Lily Hamilton and Barbara Myers

illustrated by Brendan Sellaro

To order additional copies of this book or
for book publishing information, or to contact the author:

Headline Kids
P. O. Box 52
Terra Alta, WV 26764
www.headlinekids.com

Tel: 800-570-5951
Email: mybook@headlinebooks.com
www.headlinebooks.com
www.headlinekids.com

Published by Headline Books

Headline Kids is an imprint of Headline Books

Art Direction by Ashley Teets

ISBN 0-929915-38-0
ISBN-13: 9780929915-38-8

Library of Congress Cataloging-in-Publication Data

Hamilton, Lily.
  Lily & Nana / by Lily Hamilton and Barbara Myers ; illustrated by Brendan Sellaro.
    p. cm.
  ISBN 978-0-929915-38-8
        1. Children and older people--Juvenile literature. 2. Grandparent and child--Juvenile literature.
        3. Intergenerational relations--Juvenile literature. I. Myers, Barbara, 1942- II. Sellaro, Brendan.
      III. Title. IV. Title: Lily and Nana.
  HQ784.A34H36 2011
  305.2--dc22
                                                                2010039550

PRINTED IN THE UNITED STATES OF AMERICA

Lily likes to
be with Nana.

Nana likes to
be with Lily.

Lily likes to soak in the tub.

Nana likes to wash
in the shower.

Lily likes to go to Burger King™.

Nana likes to go to lunch meetings.

Lily likes to play "Go Fish."

Nana likes to play bridge.

Lily likes to
write books.

Nana likes to read books.

Lily likes to paint the play house.

Nana likes to cut out the windows and door.

Lily likes to plant the garden.

Nana likes to
water the garden.

Lily likes to set the table for a party.

Nana likes to cook the food for a party.

Lily likes to shop at toy stores.

Nana likes to shop at department stores.

Lily likes to climb
on the monkey bars.

Nana likes to watch Lily swing on the swing.

Lily likes to play games on the computer.

Nana likes to write e-mails on the computer.

Lily likes to dress up in Nana's nightgowns.

Nana likes to sleep in her nightgowns.

Lily likes to eat cheese and crackers for a snack.

Nana likes to eat peanut butter
and crackers for a snack.

Lily likes to swim in the pool.

Nana likes to watch Lily dive into the pool.

Lily likes to be with Nana.

Nana likes to be with Lily.